Animal Classes
Insects

by Julie Murray

Dash!
LEVELED READERS

Level 1 – Beginning
Short and simple sentences with familiar words or patterns for children who are beginning to understand how letters and sounds go together.

Level 2 – Emerging
Longer words and sentences with more complex language patterns for readers who are practicing common words and letter sounds.

Level 3 – Transitional
More developed language and vocabulary for readers who are becoming more independent.

abdopublishing.com

Published by Abdo Zoom, a division of ABDO, PO Box 398166, Minneapolis, Minnesota 55439. Copyright © 2019 by Abdo Consulting Group, Inc. International copyrights reserved in all countries. No part of this book may be reproduced in any form without written permission from the publisher. Dash!™ is a trademark and logo of Abdo Zoom.

Printed in the United States of America, North Mankato, Minnesota.
052018
092018

Photo Credits: iStock, Shutterstock
Production Contributors: Kenny Abdo, Jennie Forsberg, Grace Hansen, John Hansen
Design Contributors: Dorothy Toth, Neil Klinepier

Library of Congress Control Number: 2017917509

Publisher's Cataloging in Publication Data

Names: Murray, Julie, author.
Title: Insects / by Julie Murray.
Description: Minneapolis, Minnesota : Abdo Zoom, 2019. | Series: Animal classes | Includes online resources and index.
Identifiers: ISBN 9781532122989 (lib.bdg.) | ISBN 9781532123962 (ebook) | ISBN 9781532124457 (Read-to-me ebook)
Subjects: LCSH: Insects--Juvenile literature. | Entomology--Juvenile literature. |Speciation (Biology)--Juvenile literature. | Insects--Behavior--Juvenile literature.
Classification: DDC 595.703--dc23

THIS BOOK CONTAINS RECYCLED MATERIALS

Table of Contents

Insects 4

Insect Traits 22

Glossary 23

Index 24

Online Resources 24

Insects

Insects are all around you! There are more than one million different kinds.

Insects have been on Earth for more than 400 million years!

7

Insects do not have a backbone. They have a hard covering. It is on the outside of their bodies.

9

An insect has three main body parts. It has a head, **thorax**, and an **abdomen**.

abdomen

head

thorax

Insects have six legs.
Most have two **antennae**.

antenna

13

14

Most insects have wings. Honey bees fly through the air.

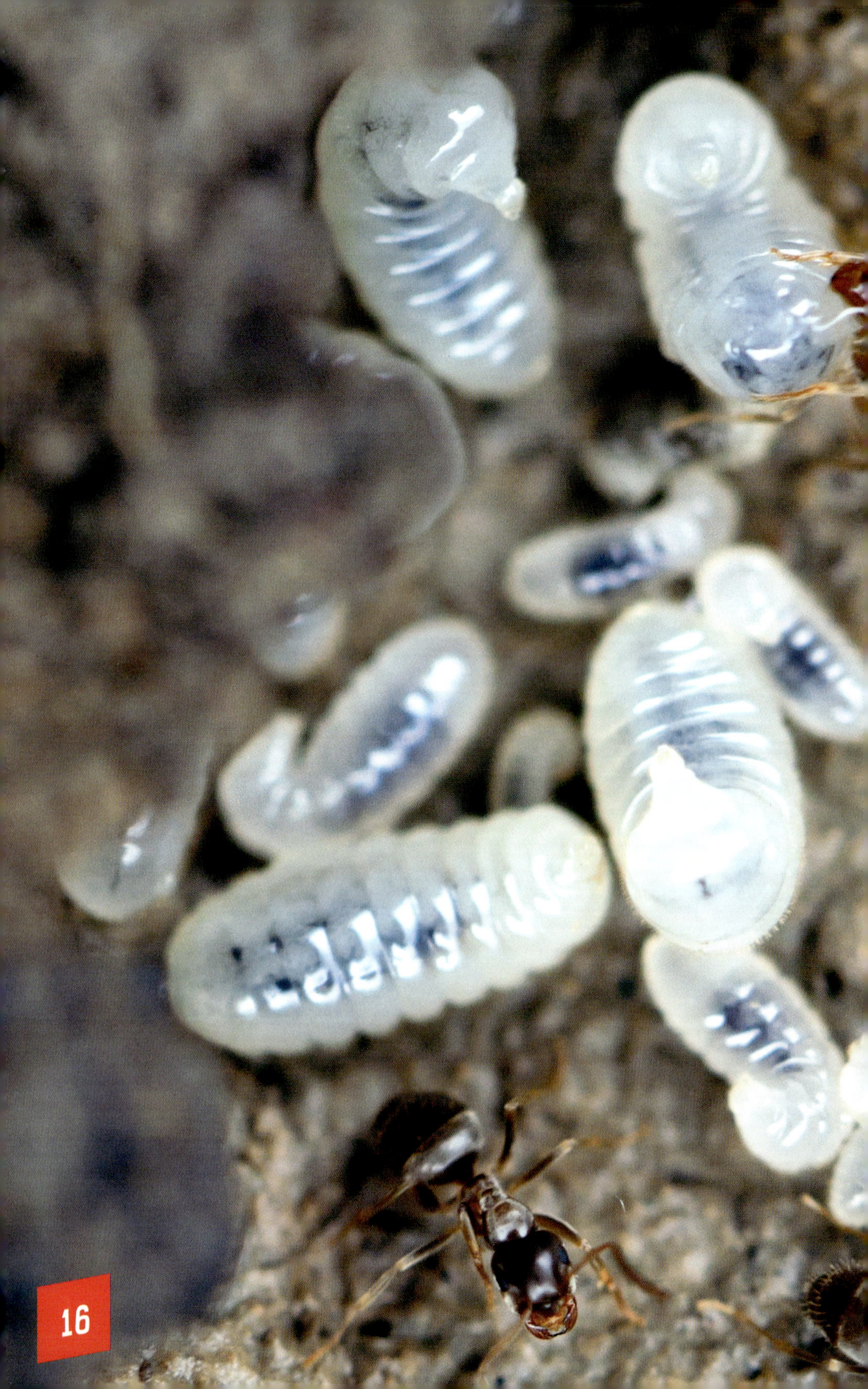

Insects lay eggs. A newly-hatched insect is a **larva**. It will grow and change into an adult.

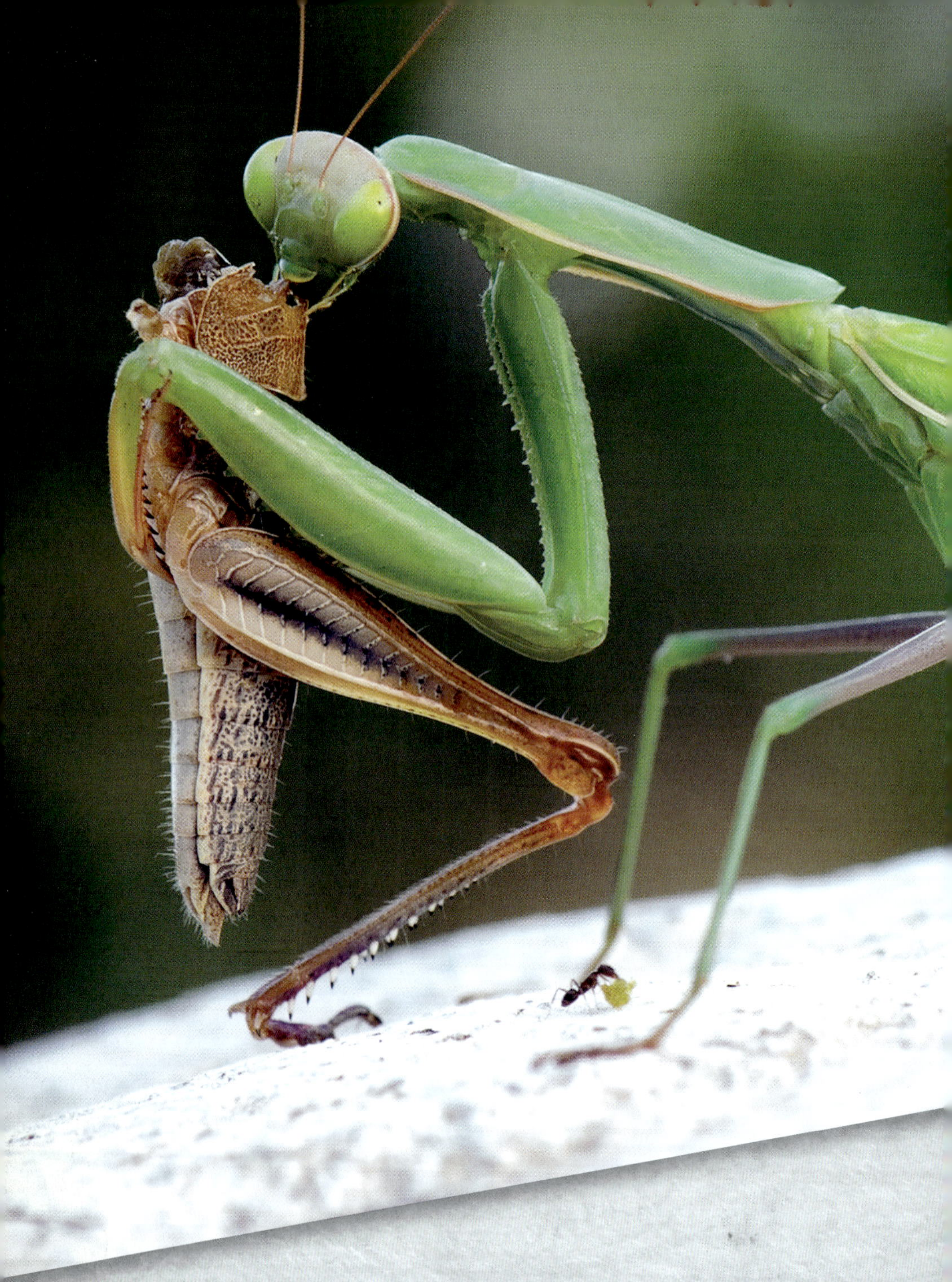

Many insects eat **nectar**, **pollen**, and plants. A praying mantis eats other insects.

Some insects are big. Titan beetles can be more than 6 inches (15 cm) long.

21

Insect Traits

- Have a hard outside covering
- Have three main body parts
- Have six legs
- Most have wings
- Change as they grow

Glossary

abdomen – the rear part of an insect's body.

antenna – one of a pair of long, thin body parts on the head of insects used to feel and smell.

larva – an insect after it hatches from an egg and before it changes into its adult form.

nectar – a sweet liquid a plant makes that attracts insects.

pollen – a fine, yellow powder made by a flowering plant.

thorax – the middle part of an insect's body.

Index

antennae 12

body 8, 10

eggs 17

food 19

honey bee 15

larva 17

legs 12

life cycle 17

praying mantis 19

size 20

species 5

titan beetle 20

wings 15

Online Resources

Booklinks
NONFICTION NETWORK
FREE! ONLINE NONFICTION RESOURCES

To learn more about insects, please visit **abdobooklinks.com**. These links are routinely monitored and updated to provide the most current information available.